"CALLING OUT ALL MEN"

A guide to manhood

By
Jeffery Alan Hill

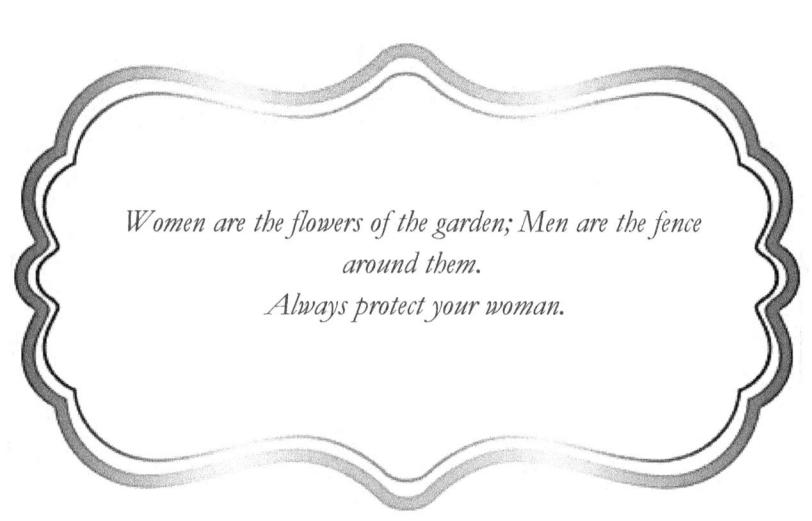

Women are the flowers of the garden; Men are the fence around them.
Always protect your woman.

About the author

Jeffery Hill is currently incarcerated in NC. He is in the process of trying to get back home to his family and back into society. He was inspired to write this book because he has watched so many young men and older men living from day to day and avoiding the responsibility of manhood. He admits that even from behind bars, he has always taken his duty as a father as far as he could in his situation. He also realizes that he can't change his past, but he can make a difference in his future and the future of others around him in a positive way. His hobbies include reading, writing, watching and playing sports.

You can contact him @ Jeffery Alan Hill, 1023873

North Carolina Department of Adult Correction
GTL Getting Out App

Acknowledgements

First and foremost, I would like to thank God because without him nothing is possible. I would like to thank my ancestors, the ones that I was blessed to meet and be around as a kid/man. To my ancestors that I never got a chance to meet, I love y'all and thanks for the sacrifices you all made so I could be here today. To my mother: I love you, and I'm sorry for any hurt I've caused you as I grew up. Thank you for still being here through it all. To my father: We never got the chance to really know one another, but at the end of the day, you're still my dad. I love you, Pops. It's still not too late. To my beautiful kids, Dynasty and Daniel Hill: There aren't enough words to put on paper to express my love and feelings. I'm sorry that my mistakes and my ignorance as a young boy caused us to be apart all these years. I was a boy, now I'm a man. To my sister Shonckia Hill, I love you more than you'll ever know.

To all my friends and family: Ashley Brown, Rogerick Williams, Willie Tyler, Mark Artest, Boot, and all the good brothers I met in prison, hold y'all's head up. Things can only get better. To my publisher: Thanks for giving me a chance. Promise not to let you down.

To anyone I may have forgotten, I apologize, don't blame it on my heart. To anybody I have hurt in any form, I'm sincerely sorry.

Peace,

Jeffrey Alan Hill

Table of Contents

Preface
PUT GOD FIRST

—●·●·●—

This is by far the most important part of this book; I am not going to sit here and try to preach to you or beat religion in your head. That is not the purpose of this book or this chapter, but you do need to know and understand that it all starts with him. Put God first in all that you do, and your blessings will come abundantly. As you read this book, you will see that everything that I've written to you is possible.

Chapter One

DEAR MOM

———◆•◆◆———

From the time we are in our mother's womb until the point that we start to so-called feeling ourselves, we are dependent on our mother. Even when we are grown and rusty, some of us are still dependent on our mothers, which is really a crying shame. Brothers, when we reach a certain age, our mothers should be able to depend on us, not the other way around. She changed your diapers, took care of you while you were still being developed, and was there on your first day of school. When you had your first heartbreak. The list goes on and on. Still, we find a way not to show our appreciation for our beautiful mothers all over the world. How can we truly love a woman if we don't even love and respect our mother? It will never happen.

Think about all the sacrifices your mother made for you as a kid. Working two, sometimes three jobs to put food on the table and a roof over your head. What about that brand new pair of shoes that had just come out? You knew and she knew that she could not afford to buy those shoes, but somehow, someway, she made that sacrifice anyway. All she asked you to do was take the trash out or wash the dishes, and you started pouting. All because you were trying to get back to your room and play a video game that SHE made the sacrifice for you so that you would be happy. Yeah, I know you are probably shaking your head right now because it sounds familiar. Didn't it? Trust me, I know because I was once that same little knuckleheaded boy. At the same time, I still obeyed her no matter how much I pouted.

A lot of boys are raised in single-parent homes, and that can influence them as they get older, because they didn't have that male role model in their lives. There ain't no love like a mother's love, but boys still need their fathers in their lives, or at least a positive role model. Our mothers still do the best they can, and a lot of us turn out to be alright men, but we need to strive to be better men. It all starts with respecting and being obedient to our mothers. Don't get me wrong, brothers, I know at times our mothers can be what we young brothers consider annoying. At the end of the day, she is still your mother. Now, in your mind, you are probably thinking. Hold up now, I'm not a child anymore, so why is this dude telling me all this? I'm saying this because it is your job to teach your sons this so they may grow into better men than you are, but we will get to that later in the book. It doesn't matter that you are grown up now, that's even better. Now you can take the time to go sit with your mother one or two days out of a week. Take her out to eat and buy her something nice. Show that appreciation to her for making all those sacrifices for you when you were still pissing in bed and running around trying to keep up with the latest fashion. Even a phone call every day or every other day just to tell her you love her. I can guarantee you it will make her day, and she will feel so much better, no matter what she may be going through. So, pick up the phone and call your mother. Nine times out of ten, you are not doing anything else anyway.

Do you remember when you were young and used to get sick? Who was always there to comfort and make things so much better? Who was the first person you called on already knew she would have the remedy for your sickness? Who did you run to when you used to think monsters were under your bed or in the closet? I could go on forever giving you examples, but I'm pretty sure you get the point, so do something about it. No matter what your religion, I know that honoring your mother and father is a golden rule. A lot of times in our lives, we as men always seem to make excuses. I'm tired, I'm busy, I have something to do, or I forget. Let me explain something to you. There is no excuse in this world for not honoring your mother. There is no excuse for constantly disrespecting your mother, no matter what the case may be.

I was talking to a lady friend the other day, and she told me how her sister disrespected her mother. They were arguing, and the sister got mad and said, "You used to be a crackhead anyway". Can you imagine how that made the mother feel? That was wrong in every sense of the word. Personally, if my sister or brother talks to my mother like that in my presence, they are going to be swallowing some teeth. It doesn't matter what your mother used to do; keep it real, it doesn't matter what she does now. At the end of the day, she is still your mother. She carried you for nine months. She went through labor pains to push you out into this world. How dare you disrespect her? You have no right at all. No matter what she is out there doing, she does it to provide for you. Growing up, I used to watch my mother being physically abused by different men. It seemed that no matter what man she brought home, eventually, he ended up putting his hands on her. I remember thinking as a child, "What is momma doing to make these men abuse her"? Of course, I would try to help, but there is nothing a 5.6-or 7-year-old can do with a grown man, so I'd have to sit back and watch and pray that it would eventually end. I bring that up because maybe your mother is in a relationship right now. I'm not telling you to disrespect her men or anything like that, but you know, sometimes go talk to him to get a feel for him, so you'll know your mom is in safe hands.

Talk to your mother about her relationship. Communication is the key in every relationship, regardless of what type of relationship it is. It could be your life, your boss, your kids, your mother, etc., you must communicate. Take the time out to listen sometimes. You will be surprised at the bond you and your mother would share if you just took the time to talk with her. It all starts with your mother, remember that. She is the first lady always, so before you can love a woman, before you get engaged, you must love your mother. You must learn from her what it takes to love a woman. Your mother is the most important lady in your life. Don't ever forget that. With that being said, love, honor, and respect her until your last breath. Once she is gone, she is gone. You don't want to live the rest of your life thinking what you should've said, what you should've done. Say it now and do it now, brothers, while you still get a chance.

Chapter Two
FROM A BOY TO A MAN

There comes a point in a man's life when enough is enough. In the bible, it says, when I was a child, I spoke like a child, I thought like a child, I reasoned like a child. When I became a man, I gave up childish ways. Brothers, don't a woman want a man who is immature and still playing games? Honestly, that isn't a man. That is a boy. If you have a dictionary, look up the word man. It is going to say something to the effect of: a male human having qualities considered characteristic of manhood. Those qualities consist of being a provider, protector, husband, lover, leader and so on. A lot of us so-called men, if asked what it takes to be a man, we really couldn't give a legit answer. Then some of us could give an answer, but in all actuality, we are being hypocritical because we know all the qualities of being a man. We talk a good game, but when it's all said and done, we don't take action. We don't take on the responsibilities of being a man. That is because we are still stuck in our childish ways. We still want to play games with our women. We haven't grown into that man mentally yet, and that's the problem. Then you have the select few who are actually men.

We know the qualities of being a man; we say what we mean and mean what we say. We let our actions pretty much speak for themselves. We are not running around here chasing 3 or 4 women. We are not neglecting our responsibilities. We are taking care of the home and doing what men do. I know and understand that being a man is a job, but that's the beauty of it. When you can look at yourself in the mirror and say with pride 'I am a man". A lot of us can't even look in the mirror, because we know we aren't anything. We are ashamed of what we have become because we know that we are destined for better. Brothers, it's still not too late. You can act and be the man that God made you to be. You already possess the physical characteristics of a man; now you've got to get the mental and spiritual characteristics. It's already in you; you just must look deep within yourself and grab hold of it.

I'll use myself for example. I am currently incarcerated, fighting for a chance to get back out into society, to be the man that God made me to be. Being in here has helped me grow into a man. Before I came to prison, I was a little boy. At the age of 14, I was running the streets, trying to hang out with the older fellas because it made me feel like a man. I was drinking whatever they were drinking and doing whatever they were doing whenever I could. Thinking that I was doing something because the older girls were interested in me. At that point in my life, living fast was cool. True indeed, I called myself a man, but I didn't think like a man. I didn't act like a man. I didn't live up to the responsibilities of a man. By the age of 19, I had one child and another on the way. I wasn't even old enough to get a real job with benefits. Therefore, I wasn't a man. It took me coming to prison to finally grow into a man, and even then, I still had the mentality of a boy for a long time. I had to grow mentally and sit down and re-evaluate myself.

A lot of times, we as men are moving too fast. We don't take time to sit down and think. Being 21 doesn't make you a man. Hell, being 45 doesn't make you a man. It's less about age and physical. A lot of times, while I am in the dayroom talking to the brothers incarcerated with me, I sit back and listen. A lot of men talk about how many women they have, how much money they have, etc. They can go on and on bragging about this and that, but confronted with the question, "What makes you a man"? They get stuck or give some random answer that doesn't make a bit of sense. I am not trying to talk down about no man, but I do want my brothers out there and in here to man up and be the men that they were destined to be. It's time to grow up and put boyish ways behind you. If you are a so-called man, then be a man, plain and simple.

Chapter Three
FAMILY IS LIFE

There is a book by Sister Souljah that I read, and in the book her main character was asked the question "What is Life"? His answer was one word: "Family".

Outside of God, family is the most important thing in life. Friends come and go every day. You meet different people on a regular basis. Friends turn their backs on you in your darkest moment. Family can never change. You might fall out with a family member for a long time, but that still doesn't change the fact that y'all are family. Brothers, this chapter is very important, and I want y'all to know and understand the importance of this chapter. Without family, we are lost. No man wants to be alone at all. If, for some reason, you don't have a family, you can start your own family. It's not too late. When you meet that special lady and make her your wife, you've taken the first step in the process of starting a family. When the time is right and you are both ready, you can make or adopt babies. Whatever the situation calls for is entirely up to y'all. The thing is, once those babies arrive, being a man comes into play.

Now that your wife and you have kids, it is your responsibility to provide for and protect not only the kids but your wife as well. You are the man of the house, so a lot of the pressure is on you. Nothing hurts me more than to see a man, or should I say a so-called man, turn his back on his kids. You helped create them, so now you must help raise them. A lot of our children do not reach their full potential because they don't have their father figure in their lives. This isn't to take anything away from our women who are single parents, because I salute you and admire you for what you do. Can you imagine if our kids were raised with their fathers in their lives on a regular basis? It is a fact that kids who are raised with both parents have a higher success rating in life as opposed to those raised in single-parent homes. True indeed, a lot of kids have grown to be successful despite being raised in single-parent homes. To have that father in their lives makes a big difference. It's time to break the cycle, men and take care of home. The joy you will feel in your heart is real, knowing you are the man God created you to be. He put you here to take care of your family.

How would you feel if your son were to join a gang? How would you feel if your daughter were pimped out by some random man? Yeah, I know, you wouldn't like it at all. Think about this: when our kids can't get that love from their father, who do they turn to? Your son joins a gang because now he sees someone he can look up to. The leader of that gang is now his idol or role model. Your daughter can't get the love she longs for, so who does she turn to? She allows different men to use her, use her body, because she is looking for security and love. The security and love you are supposed to give. You are supposed to be that role model for your son. Your kids are supposed to come to you when they have doubts or when they feel like they can't talk to anybody else. Your kids are the most precious thing you could ever have in life, not money, clothes, cars, etc. When you have kids, automatically, a change is supposed to come over you.

Having kids is a part of growing into manhood as well. It doesn't matter whether you and the mother are getting along. Neither does it matter whether you and the mother are still in a relationship. You planted the seed inside of her, and she carried it and gave birth to a new life. It is your responsibility to raise that child. A lot of us look for excuses not to be in a child's life. The number one excuse that I hear all the time is "My baby mama is tripping, or she won't let me see my child". Yeah, that is a lame, pathetic excuse for a man. Nobody, not even the mother, can keep you from your child if you want to be in your child's life. If you are working and don't have a haphazard home, the court system will allow you to have joint custody of your child. There again, it shouldn't even come to the court system. If you meet a "WOMAN" and the two of you end up having a child, she is going to push you to be in that child's life, whether y'all are together or not. So, you can miss me with all those excuses as to why you aren't in your kid's life. I'm telling you, brother, after God, family is the most important thing in the world. Family is life, and without family, life has absolutely no purpose.

Chapter Four

LOVING OUR WOMEN

———— •◦• ————

Women were created for a man to love unconditionally, not for us to abuse or hurt. There is nothing like a strong woman. I know you have heard the saying "behind every man is a good woman". But I say" beside every man there is a great woman". Women are our backbone.

Women are the reason you cleaned up and put on that new oil/cologne. No matter what you say, you cannot deny the fact that women are what motivate us. The problem is that a lot of us aren't satisfied with one woman. That is and will always be a big problem until we truly man the hell up. We can have the sweetest, caring, loving woman, and we will still cheat on her and hurt her for a few minutes of pleasure. I ask guys all the time, would they throw away a lifetime of happiness over one night of pleasure? Brothers, if you have that special lady in your life, you must hold on to her. Love her unconditionally, protect her, provide for her, be her best friend, and be there when she needs you the most. Our women don't get the love, affection, appreciation or the credit they deserve.

Can you imagine having to endure what our women must endure? I know I couldn't imagine having to experience what our

12

women experience daily. When was the last time you opened a door for your woman? When was the last time you rubbed her feet after a long day at work? When was the last time you had her bath water warm and ready when she came home from a long, stressful day? When was the last time you simply catered to your woman? Why does she always have to cater to you as opposed to you catering to her? If you can't answer any of those questions that I just asked, then there is a problem, but it isn't too late. You can start now; it is better to change now than to stay set in your ways. I know a lot of brothers are thinking along the lines of "man, I am not the romantic type". Well, if that is the case, Brother, you'd better get with the program, cause what you don't do for her, there is somebody else that will. You must continue to court your woman, no matter how long y'all have been together. Do you remember all you had to endure to win her? I am pretty sure you had to court her back then. Well, the same things you did to get her are the same things you must do to keep her. A lot of marriages/ relationships fail because the couples become stagnant, or they fall into a routine. That is the worst thing you could do in a relationship. You must add spice to your relationship. Keep your woman off balance and in suspense about what your next move is going to be. If you do this, you will see how much smoother your relationship will be. The sex will be better, and the energy between both of you will always be positive. Trust me, brothers, it doesn't take much. Women love the little things the most. It's about taking the time to think of the small things that matter most to them. Don't get it twisted now. We all know women love to shop and they love jewelry, but I promise you, if you were to do something as simple as buying her a just because card with a nice message inside, along with a single rose, that would mean so much more than a shopping spree. I'll tell you again, "it's the simple/small things that matter the most.

I read this book by Nicolas Sparks called "The Wedding". If you don't know who he is, he is an author who writes romance novels, and most of his books have been made into movies. In this book, the man forgot his and his wife's anniversary, which we all know is the ultimate no-no when it comes to women. Once he realized he had forgotten, he knew he had to make it right. He began to court his wife all over again. I bring that up because it doesn't matter 30, 50 or 75 years old, you must keep the fire burning in your relationship. It's okay to make mistakes, don't get me wrong. We are human, so we are entitled to make mistakes. The thing is, don't continue to make the same mistakes repeatedly. Eventually, that gets old, and she isn't going to continue to tolerate it.

Do you remember back in the day when you were in middle or high school? You used to write love letters to your girlfriend. When was the last time you wrote your woman a love letter, if you have ever written one at all? I'm telling you, man, it's the small things. I can't emphasize that enough. Can you imagine the look on your woman's face if she came home and found a love letter that you took the time to write to her? I promise you it will make a difference in your relationship, and you'll see a change for the better. These are just little ideas that I'm giving you. Don't nobody know your woman the way you do, so maybe something different will work for you. My point is that you need to love, respect and honor your woman, because once she is gone, you might realize that you lost the best thing to ever happen to you.

Chapter Five
OUR COMMUNITY

Men, we all play a major role in our community. If you don't think you do, then it's time to change your way of thinking right now. Our communities are falling apart because we are not taking the time to uplift our communities. We are so busy focusing on other things, and our communities are being destroyed right in front of our eyes, and we don't even see it. It is time for you to look around your community and see all the destruction and negativity that's going on. People are selling drugs, prostitution, gangbanging, murder, robbery, just to name a few, but I'm here to tell you that as a man, you can bring about a change. You must lead by example with your ways and actions. Don't focus on the negativity that is going on around you. Instead, focus on what you can do in a positive way to create change. Don't be one of those brothers who made it out of the hood and never go back. You made it out for a reason, and despite what you may believe, you must give back. Now, maybe you are thinking, "What has the hood even done for me"? It's not about what the hood has or hasn't done for you. Those are your roots, and it's about what you are gonna do for the hood, or should I say your community? You can motivate a child or another adult in your community with your positive and caring actions. Have a cookout for the entire community. Do some type of volunteer work, like helping the elderly. You don't have to be rich or make it to the big time to give back to your community. Talking to the youth gives them some type of motivation, also so they will want more out of life.

You are a man, and people will always follow a man's lead if he is leading in the right and positive direction. You were born to be a leader. When you came out of your mother's womb, it was predestined for you to make a positive impact on the world. You don't have to be a professional athlete, rapper, lawyer or doctor. Just be you. Don't ever change who you are. There are other brothers out there who will help you clean your community. By cleaning up your community, I mean starting up activities that the kids can participate in after school or during spring or summer break. Give them something to look forward to that will keep them away from the street. I promise you that if you can only change one child's life at a time, that in itself is good enough. Our kids are our future, and that child who could one day become president could possibly be in your community waiting on you to push them and have their back. You never know what the future may hold, but I do know this: if you play a major role in anybody's success in your community, whether it is a child or not, you've done your deed, and that person will never forget you.

How many times have you seen celebrities who made it and not once give back to their community? It happens more times than not. You don't have to be that celebrity brother. Giving back to your community, in my opinion, is a major part of being a man. It shows your growth and maturity. It shows that you care not only about yourself and your family, but you care about others as well. A few good men could make all the difference, brother. Be that difference maker for once in your life, but be that difference maker for something positive. You've heard the saying "you reap what you sow"; well, reap the benefits for uplifting your community. You will feel so much better about yourself, and it will give you peace of mind and heart knowing you made a difference.

Chapter Six
KARMA

—•••—

"What goes around, comes around", we are all familiar with this phrase. At some point in our lives, somebody has told us this. No matter what it is in life, it matters what you do in life. You get what you give in life. You will always be faced in life with the results of what you've done to or for another person. It doesn't matter if it was physical or mental. Your thoughts, your words or your deeds will always come back around full circle. Let me be clear on something, though, brother, a lot of people are confused when it comes to karma. They automatically assume it is something negative, but that is not always the case. You have "good karma" as well as "bad karma". The thing is, karma has a purpose, and its purpose is to teach us a lesson so we can learn from it. It's all a part of growing into a man. Are you familiar with cause and effect? Every action has a reaction. It's like whatever your thought, desire or purpose may be, that's your creation. Basically, you create your destiny through cause and effect. Everything you have is because it is what you want. Everything that you experience in life reflects what you ask for. Let me give you a better example of what I am talking about. Let's say that you are finally married and you love your wife more than anything in this world. One day, she decides to run off with John Doe. It's the worst feeling you have experienced in your life. You can't function at all. You can't think straight if you get yourself together and think about what you've done to deserve this. You'll remember that time back in the day when you were a so-called "playa" and you had sex with your neighbor's wife, or that time you stole some man's wife from him? It isn't anything but karma coming in full circle.

So now I know a lot of people are thinking, "What does karma have, if anything, to do with this book"? Karma has everything to do with this book and you as a man. As a man, it is up to you to control whether or not you have good karma or bad karma. If you are reading this book and taking the necessary steps to become a better man, you are paving your way for the future to have good karma when it comes back around. You must always stay in a positive mind frame, brother. Don't allow negative things around you to determine your actions. It still goes back to karma. If you are constantly thinking negative thoughts, then, as a result, negative things are going to happen in your life. I know it is always hard to stay in a positive frame of mind. We are human, so of course, we are going to have times when we are in a negative state of mind. Just remember that you are sending those negative thoughts into the universe, and they will come back around full circle. Maybe not now, it could be a year or two from now or even later, but it will come back around. You can change it by having thoughts about love, peace and happiness.

Send those positive thoughts into the universe, and as a result, you will have the love, peace and happiness that you crave for in your life. Everything starts with a thought, brother. Remember to always be mindful of what you are thinking. You have the power to control your destiny, brother. Just make sure you do it in a constructive way. I know that it is a cutthroat world out there, but that doesn't have to be you. Don't look for shortcuts or try to find the easy way out. Remember, you are going to get what you give. Through hard work and determination, you will make it. Anything worth having doesn't come easy. That's simply a law of life. What type of world would it be like if everybody had everything given to them so easily? It would be a world of madness and chaos. Men, your life is what you make it. It is up to us to choose what we will manifest into our lives. Just remember that whatever it is that you choose, the law will bring it back to you. Let me break it down a little deeper so you can get a full understanding. Let's say someone breaks into your home and steals some jewelry or something of value. Ok, you are thinking, "I've never broken into anyone's home, but see that's the thing. You didn't break into their home, but you have treated someone unfairly. Maybe someone needed you at a crucial moment of their life, but you refused to be there for them. Karma doesn't mean that the act will be the exact same thing. It's about the spirit, your spirit to be specific, and the spirit involved will be the same. Do you follow me? If you were to clean somebody out of money, or if you were to con somebody out of property, what spirit do you think that is? It is the spirit of selfishness. When it comes back, and believe you me, it will come back. Remember that even though those acts were different, they may come back in a different form. With that being said, when you think as a man should thinketh, and you do the things as a man should do, you will get the results that a man is supposed to get. It is entirely up to you, brother, and it all starts in your mind.

Chapter Seven
THE SYSTEM

This chapter is more than likely to rattle a few cages and possibly offend some people. If I cared, then I wouldn't have written it. Brothers, the system is designed to bring you under and keep you away from your family. If you have ever been in the system, then you know exactly what I am talking about. If you've never been in the system, I tip my hat to you, and I pray that you never have to experience it. I've been a part of the system for the past 20 years, and it is my biggest regret in life. Can you imagine not getting the chance to raise your kids? To see your kids grow up in life while you are behind bars is a feeling no man should ever feel. I am not going to sit here and pretend or fake the funk like I am an angel, because I am not. The way this system is set up is wrong. People make mistakes, truly indeed. I will go so far as to say some people are supposed to be behind bars. That doesn't mean that everyone who is are bad person. I have met some good, sharp and positive brothers here, but that is not the point of this chapter. This chapter is a warning to all men out there. If you are indulging in foolishness, it's time to change before it's too late and you get caught up in the system.

My intentions are not to take anything away from lawyers out there who are sincere in their job. A lot of times, brothers are assigned to a public defender. For those that are unfamiliar, that is a lawyer that the court assigns to you because you are unable to afford one. Once this happens, brothers, depending on your chances, you are doomed. Before you know it, you are on a bus headed to prison for X amount of time. More than likely, you received more time than was necessary. Now you are thinking, how can I get back into court and make this right? The catch to that is you must go back through that same system that puts you there in the first place.

Those so-called friends that you thought were gonna "keep it real" with you are nowhere to be found. That so-called "woman" that you called your girl jumped the fence as soon as she heard how much time you have. Family isn't family anymore. They don't want anything to do with you. You are a disgrace to the family name. Now, this may not be the case for some brothers who get caught in the system. For the most part, that's exactly how it is. Now you are surrounded by murderers, rapist, pedophiles and all types of criminals. You are looking around, knowing in your heart you aren't supposed to be here, but you are, and now you have to learn to adapt to your environment. Brothers, I'm pleading with you and warning you that no amount of money in this world is worth ever getting caught up in the system. At the end of the day, that's what it boils down to. You were after money, and it landed you in prison. Let's fast forward, and now you are finally out. You paid society for the crime you committed. Now you are finally free (or so you think). You must check in and pay your probation officer for the next $9 - 12$ months. How can you do that when nobody hires you? You never want to return to that hellhole again, so day after day you get up and job hunt. You fill out applications everywhere. You aren't choosy, you'll take a job anywhere. Just when you think that you've caught a break and gonna be hired, they run a background check on you and see that you have a criminal record. "We will give you a call" is what they say. You know in your heart that call is never gonna come. After a while, you are angry and resort to what you do best, "crime". Brothers, what I just described to you is exactly what happens to a lot of men who have been a part of the system. It's designed like a revolving door. It's set up so that once you've been trapped in it, you keep coming back. It's a cycle that goes on for generations, but it can be broken, brothers. If you are living the way you are supposed to be living, then this doesn't apply to you. My advice to you is to continue to work hard and take care of your responsibilities. That way, you will never get trapped in the system. To the brothers who have been caught in the system, it's time for a change. It's time to break the cycle. No matter how many times you keep getting denied for that job, you must keep pressing on. You can't give up and accept defeat, because if you do, you've let the system win. There is somebody out there who's willing to give you a chance. The thing is, when you get that chance, don't blow it. Show your employer that you are a determined, hardworking man. Don't settle, though, because you can start your own business, but I will get into that in the next chapter.

My point is you must take advantage of every opportunity when it is presented to you. A lot of us use the system as an excuse for why we can't make progress in life. Truthfully, that's not an excuse; that should give you motivation. I know that it's hard and I know that it's unfair, but if you call yourself a man, then you can overcome that adversity. They want you to give up and resort to crime. They know that the statistics are stacked against you, so they throw you back into society with no education or any type of program to help get you started.

In the prison system, they have taken away certain classes, so you can't take them anymore. Sure, there are still some classes available, but as far as you getting a legitimate degree or trade, that's almost over. They want you to go back to society deaf, dumb and blind. That's why there aren't as many classes available anymore. It's time to wake up my brothers. You must open your eyes and see what's going on in front of you. Once the system has that chokehold on you, it's hard to get out. I'm not saying it's impossible cause I've seen brothers leave prison and become successful. You control your own destiny. Remember, you must put the work in and not be lazy. To the brothers who are reading this that has never been a part of the system, this chapter is still useful for you because you can now see how the system affects you if you ever get caught up. Don't be another statistic, brother, be what God created you to be.

Chapter Eight
KNOW YOUR WORTH

Men, we have so much potential and so much talent, but often we don't tap into it because we honestly don't know our worth. How many times have you heard as a child that 'you are never going to be anything'? It doesn't matter where it comes from or who it came from. A lot of us have been affected by those negative words all the way into adulthood. Anytime we fail at a task, we flashback to when somebody told us that, but you must snap out of it. Don't allow what the next person says or thinks to determine your success or accomplishments. When you get up and look in the mirror every day, what is it that you see? I'm not talking from a physical aspect, but a spiritual aspect. A lot of men are lost because they don't know themselves. When they look in the mirror, they don't recognize themselves. Why is that? The answer is quite simple, because they are not spiritually in tune with themselves. I'm not talking from a religious aspect either, so don't assume that.

For you to know your self-worth, you have to be spiritually in tune with yourself. Do you love yourself? Yeah, I know that you are probably saying and thinking. Of course, I love myself. What type of question is that? I ask you because some of us say that we love ourselves, but we really don't, or at least our actions say otherwise. Actions speak louder than words, right? Through your words, you say that you love yourself, but you are poisoning your body with hard drugs, drinking alcohol, smoking cigarettes, etc. Your body is your temple, and eventually, if you continue to indulge in these things, your body will wear down. I'm not telling you how to live your life, or what you can or cannot do. That's not my place, and I have no authority to do so. I just want you to please be mindful, brother. We are worth so much, but we never realize it because we aren't conscious of our potential. It is easy for us to turn away from the task of knowing our self-worth because we don't realize the importance or fully understand what it means. Hopefully, by the time you finish this chapter and this book, you will understand that knowing your self-worth is the most important thing you must do. It should be your number one priority. Before you can love anybody else, you must love yourself. Do you know who the most important person in your world is? **<u>YOU!</u>**

You have unlimited potential, and you will realize that once you tap into it. Don't compare yourself to the next man. That is not important at all. Every human is different in a variety of ways. Just remember that we are all created equal. What makes you joyful? What makes you comfortable deep within? What gives you peace? These are your true wants, needs and desires that come deep from within. You must search for the answers to these questions. I or any other person in this world can't answer this for you. There are two parts to you. You have your lower self and your higher self. When you are in your lower self you are surrounded by chaos, madness, and confusion. Fear, greed, shame, lust, and selfishness are just a few characteristics of your lower self. When you get into your lower self, anything is subject to happen. You cannot allow their negative characteristics to control you or your mind. When you are in your lower self, things are going to constantly go wrong in your life. You must change your thought process. A lot of times, we wonder why we just can't get it right or why bad stuff continues to happen. But it is because we are in our lower self. It all goes back to putting that negative energy into the universe. As long as you are in your lower self, you'll never get far, and you'll never know your worth, and if you never know your worth, how can you get your kids or your woman to know their worth? It's impossible, brother, you won't get them to see their worth. But on the flip side of that, as you have your lower self, you have your higher self. Patience, humbleness, loyalty, gentleness, and kindness are just a few characteristics of your higher self. Can you imagine what the world would be like if every man would practice having these characteristics and every positive characteristic in being in his higher self? How often do you go to bed at peace? You must find that peace within yourself. It all goes with knowing your worth. Do you think a woman wants a man who doesn't know his self-worth? Don't no grown woman want a man that doesn't know his worth. It isn't her place to awaken this in you. You should already know it. That way, when you meet her, you can help her realize her worth. Let me tell you a little story about when I met my queen. She was lost. She didn't even realize that she was a queen. She didn't know her worth. Not to take anything away from her, because she was still a wonderful woman. But at the same time, she had been dealing with so many so-called men who were in their lower selves that they couldn't uplift her, for the simple fact that they couldn't uplift themselves. They didn't know their worth, so there was no way that they could get her to open her eyes and see her worth. But as time went on, after we met and we bonded and spent time getting to know one another, she realized her worth. Today, my woman knows that she is a queen, and no man or woman could even break her spirit again because she knows her worth. My point in telling you this is that if you look deep within yourself, you will find everything you are searching for, and you can help your woman find it as well within herself. Don't be one of those brothers who let their talents go to waste. Don't be one of those brothers who lays up with a woman depending on her to take care of him. If you are one of those brothers, you are absolutely low, and you definitely don't know your worth. You might spend the rest of your life wondering "what if". So, get up and look in the mirror. Look yourself in the eyes and ask yourself. Do I know my worth?. If you can answer that question truthfully, then you have taken a positive step. Now all you must do is apply yourself. You control your own destiny, brothers, and it all starts with knowing your worth. I know my worth; that's how I was able to help my woman, and you can do the same.

Chapter Nine

MR. CASANOVA

Are you one of those brothers who think you are God's gift to every woman? Do you think that you can get any woman that you desire? If you are one of those brothers who think like this, it's time for you to wake up and snap out of it. Every woman doesn't want you, no matter how handsome you may be. A grown woman is looking for more than the physical anyway. She wants stability and someone who is mentally and spiritually on her level. You are not in high school anymore, brother. Back then, it was cool to see how many notches you could get under your belt. You were a teenager with raging hormones just like every other teenager. But that was 15, 20 years ago? Fast forward to today. You don't have any business still running around like a teenager chasing skirts. I understand if you are going on different dates looking for somebody you click with. There is a difference between dating and just sleeping around with random women. There are consequences to all of our actions. Let's say you meet a woman in the grocery store or the mall one day. The two of you start a conversation, and you can already feel the sexual energy between the two of you. So, you end up having sex. After the sex, it's over, right? Wrong! She is calling you up a few weeks later to inform you that she is pregnant with your child. Now, either one or two things are going to happen. One, you are going to take responsibility for your recklessness and be there throughout her pregnancy and get a DNA test done when she has the baby or two, you are going to go into denial, saying I used a condom, there is no way that the baby is mine. Now here comes the drama. She has the baby; the child is yours, and now you realize this woman is crazy and won't let you see the child and put you on child support. (No disrespect to women because I know all you aren't like that) But brother, do you see my point? All of this is unnecessary drama and headaches in your life. How about you meet this same woman, and y'all have mind-blowing sex. A few weeks or even a few months later, for some reason, you are sick and can't figure out the problem. You schedule a doctor's appointment. After getting some tests done on yourself, it has been confirmed that you are HIV positive. Now your entire world has come apart. You can't really pinpoint who gave it to you because you are a "playa", you are "Mr. Casanova, God's gift to women". Brothers, it's time to grow up and slow down. These scenarios that I have described to you are very much real and could happen to you. There comes a point in a man's life when enough is enough. It goes back to what I wrote earlier out of the bible. "When I was a child, I spoke like a child, I thought like a child, I reasoned like a child. When I became a man, I gave up childish ways" (1 Corinthians 13:11). Are you worried about what your friends are going to think? You are the "Casanova Crew," and settling down isn't soon for some of y'all. If these are the type of friends you are hanging out with, it's time for you to part ways. Do you want to die alone? Look at yourself in the mirror and ask yourself this question. The obvious answer is no. Nobody wants to die alone. Nobody wants to keep waking up every morning to different women or to an empty bed. God made man and woman to be as one. He didn't create it so you would go through life all alone. So, stop running around, sleeping with different women, pretending to be God's gift to every woman you see. If you continue loving like this, you'll end up finding yourself alone, living with so many "what ifs". It's time to tighten up, brother, turn that "playa" card in and be a man. Lead by example through your ways and actions. You never know who's watching. Your ways and actions could help another person someday. They may want to follow in your footsteps, so let's get it together, men.

Chapter Ten
STREETS KEEP CALLING

───●·•·●───

This book isn't just written for one particular type of man. I titled this book "Calling Out All Men" because in talking to every male on this earth, it doesn't matter what your race is, your religion or where you're from. This book is directed toward ALL MEN. I know it's a lot of brothers out there who are still caught up in the street life, hence the title for this chapter. I don't knock no man for how he provides for his family, not to say that I'm encouraging criminal activity, but I know there are some intelligent brothers out there in the streets, so I wanted to dedicate a chapter to y'all as well. So, if you are reading this chapter and it reflects you, then I hope it will change your outlook on things, because you know, just like I know, there are only two endings if you are caught up in street life. The first ending is death, and the second ending is prison. There is no third choice. Either you're in or you're out. Oftentimes, it all goes back to our childhood. Men turn to the streets because we didn't have that positive father figure in our lives, so we looked up to the next best thing in our eyes, which was that hustler who drives the fancy car with all the beautiful women or that gang member who put fear in everyone's heart. What happened to them in the end, though? A lot of us are prideful and have huge egos, but I have seen men killed or go to war over something as simple as their pride and egos. We are quick to say we are not working for minimum wage or we are not working for another man, slaving 40 hours a week just to live paycheck to paycheck. When you think and talk like that, it's only your pride and ego talking. We'd rather throw stones at the penitentiary standing on the block all day with our so-called "homies". Since this chapter is for the street dudes, let's keep it real. There is no need to sugarcoat anything. Those same "homies" on the block with you are the same "homies" who get on the stand and testify in front of a grand jury. Now you are in prison for 15 to 20 years away from your family because you lived by the "street code". Your homie is now trying to sleep with your girl, who is on to the next baller. Don't nobody pick up the phone when you call. You had all that money in the streets, now you can't buy yourself toothpaste or deodorant cause you've given all your money to a lawyer. Your kids are now fatherless, so what do they do now? Your son turns to the streets for guidance, your daughter ain't got nobody to give her the game, so she falls for the slick-talking dude who is only after one thing. You are in prison, and you are hearing rumors about your kids. There isn't anything you can do, though, so now you are stressing over this. Do you remember all those times you were out hustling and hugging the block? You never noticed that your kids were paying attention, soaking it all in. So, what they saw you doing in their minds is the proper lifestyle. Brothers, kids are very observant when you think they aren't watching and listening, they are. So, it's up to you to school them and teach them differently. Give your daughter the game so you ain't got to worry about that slick talking pimp. You must lead by example for your kids. Believe it or not, a lot of little boys out there want to grow up and be like daddy. So, if he sees you hustling and carrying guns, what do you think he's gonna do? Brother, the streets don't have love for anybody. It's a dog-eat-dog world out there. Every man for himself. There is a better way for you, brother.

I'm tired of hearing all the excuses for why we as men are still in the streets. We are constantly complaining that nobody will hire us, or we can make more in one day on the streets as opposed to 40 hours working a job. Do you want to live the rest of your life in fear? You worried about that stick-up kid that's been laying everybody down, or you worried about the police running up in your spot. It's time to tighten up and get it together. If you are reading this, you are one of the fortunate ones who still have a chance. It's not too late to make things right in your life. A lot of us fear change because we worry about what our "homies" are going to think, but change is always good if it is for the better. I'd rather live paycheck to paycheck and be at peace than be rich but in constant fear of the police or somebody hurting my family over blood money. God put you on earth for a purpose. Trust me, brother, he didn't put you here to sell drugs, rob, steal, or kill. That's something that you chose to do. Everybody has a gift; everybody has a purpose. Look deep within yourself and find out what the purpose is, brother. You'll be surprised at all the good things that will start to happen in your life. You must be patient, though. Things aren't going to happen for you overnight. Through hard work, discipline and dedication, you'll be alright. If you are not going to change for yourself, you at least owe it to your kids and your family. I'm not here to judge you or anybody else in this world. That's not my intention or my purpose in life. I'm just trying to open up your eyes, brothers. Remember what I said, the streets don't love nobody. You can't beat the game. In the end, it'll catch up to you. Maybe not now, but eventually it will. The choice is yours, brother.

Chapter Eleven
EDUCATION

In this day in time, it's hard to get anywhere without an education. It's even harder for people with an education to find or keep a steady job. I've talked to people who attended college for four years, have degrees and a master's and still can't find any type of work. But it's important still to have an education. At least get your high school diploma or GED. A lot of kids growing up don't really understand the importance of getting their education. They see the professional athlete and the rappers, actors and so forth, and that's what they aspire to be, but that isn't reality. Only a very select few get lucky and make a career out of the things I just named. To play sports in high school or college, now I believe you must have a certain GPA. I know it was like that when I was in high school. Brothers, not only do we have to educate ourselves, but we have to teach our youth the importance of education. Your son or daughter could be the top recruit in the state, but you still need to stress the importance of education to them. They could have a career-ending injury or anything. Then what are they gonna do? They are lost now because they have invested all their time and energy in making it to the pros. Now they don't have a career to fall back on. I'm not saying that they can't make it, but it is a long shot. So, you have to keep them prepared. A lot of us won't even take the time to help our kids with their homework, or we are too busy to help them prepare for that test they have coming up. But do you realize the importance of taking time to sit down and do this? Not only are you helping them in their education, but it is also a bonding period. How many men out there are doing this? I guarantee that if you conduct a survey, the numbers would be embarrassing. Things like doing this help our kids not just on an educational level, but they also help them mentally as well. They can sit back and reflect on how Daddy helped me pass that test. All of this is a part of your job as a man. We are too quick to get "mama" to help, but we should help as well. This comes with growing and maturing. A lot of times, schools aren't educating our kids on everything. This is not to take anything away from teachers because I know a lot of y'all take pride in your job and are really trying to help the youth, but some things the "school system" isn't going to allow you to educate the youth on. Personally, brothers, I think we should educate our youth more on black history. It doesn't matter if you are black, white, Hispanic or any other race. You should still educate your kids on black history. If you aren't familiar with it, then you need to be educated as well. There is so much racism in the world today because people don't know their history. They only go by what is embedded in them as a youth. You can break that cycle as well through education. A lot of people don't want to hear the truth. They fear the truth, and that's why our youth are growing up lost and confused. It's time to wake up, though, brothers. Do your own research and teach your kids so they won't be one of the lost and confused. When is the last time you read your child a bedtime story? Yeah, I know, probably never right! Believe it or not, that is educating them as well. It's the simple thing like this that matters. You can educate your kids in so many ways. You probably think that what you are doing isn't education, but it is, brother. If you read to a child, preach to a child, discipline your child, it's all education, brother! As your children get older and have kids of their own, they will take the same lessons you taught them and teach their kids. Hopefully, you'll still be around, and you can teach your grandkids as well. At some point, brothers, change has got to come. Why not be the one to start it? You have grown men who can't even read in this world today. Why is that? It's sad, but it is true. I'm around them myself every day. You don't want your kids to be one of them, do you? If not, then take the initiative, do something about it. You'd be surprised by the bond between you and your kids if you would just read/ study with them for one hour out of the day. Now I'm not going to sit up here and act like I am the perfect father because I am far from it. I've been locked up all my kids' entire lives, and I do know what it takes to establish that bond/relationship with your kids. My kids know how much they mean to me, and they know the importance of education because I preach it to them over the phone and in letters. So, brothers, if you are reading this and you are incarcerated, that isn't an excuse either. While you are sitting around watching TV, playing games or getting caught up in prison politics, you could be using that time to reach out and educate your kids. Your kids are the most important thing in your life outside of God. So educate them in everything. Educate yourselves as well because you can't educate your kids or any youth if you aren't educated yourself. Don't be one of the deaf, dumb, or blind brothers.

Chapter Twelve
CHOICES

Life is about choices. You make good choices, and you make bad choices. Sometimes the choices you make can have a lifelong effect on you as well as your family. A lot of men today are still suffering the consequences because of the choices they made in the past. When God created you, he gave you a choice. You could either live a righteous life or you could submit to your weaknesses and live an evil life. You still had a choice. Let me ask you a question, and I want you to really think about it before you answer. Do you believe you created your destiny, or do you believe it was already written? There is no right or wrong answer; it is really opinionated. I'm going to give you my opinion, and maybe it will help you think about your choices in the future. I believe that we create our own destiny through our thoughts, ways and actions. Basically, you create your own destiny from the choices you make. Let me use myself as an example. God didn't bring me into this world just so I could come to prison. He had a plan for me, and he still does, but by my making the choice to commit a crime, I ended up going to prison. There is no evil in God. Anything that isn't Godly that we do is of our own free will. I chose to run with the wrong crowd on my own. Now I am paying for the choices that I made. A lot of times, we make bad choices, then the first thing we do is call on God. When he doesn't answer when we want him to, we continue to make bad choices. The choices we make determine our fate; whether you believe that or not is entirely up to you. Once again, it comes down to choices. Whether you believe it or not, that's your choice. When you look back on your life and say I should've done this or that differently, you are saying you should've made a different choice. The thing is, though, we can't dwell on the past. That is done and over with. You will never get yesterday back, so you must focus on the future. There is still a lot of life in you to live, and you have a choice today about what to do about your future. Just don't continue to make the wrong decisions or let anyone influence you to make the wrong decisions. Being a man comes with a lot of responsibility, brothers. A major part of that responsibility is making the right choices for your life. Earlier, I mentioned that not only do your choices affect you, but your family as well. Your family is one of your most important responsibilities, so you must make sure you make the right choices. This will have a positive effect on their lives. Once you man up and become a real man with a family, you must ask yourself, will I continue to choose the path that I've chosen in the past, or will I find a new path and make better choices? If you are going to transform your life in a positive way, this is the question that you need to ask yourself, because if you really want to change your life, you must change your choices. You've heard the saying "Actions speak louder than words". It's easy to say out of your mouth that you want to make better choices and change your life, but what are you doing about it? True indeed, everything does start with a thought, but after this thought, you must manifest it into actual being. I know that it takes time to create change, but do it, don't just say it. Also, don't keep living in the past. Don't be one of those brothers that's constantly saying I should've done this or I could've done that. I am surrounded by so many of these types of brothers every day. We can't change anything about the past; we can't go back and undo any of the choices we made. Can you imagine what the world would be like if we could? God gave us free will to make our own choices so we could learn.

You learn from your mistakes, or at least you are supposed to. Not only do you learn from the bad choices you made, but you can also learn from the good choices as well. It's a growing process for brothers. It's time to make a positive transformation. The choice is yours, choose wisely!

Chapter Thirteen
IGNORANCE

The other day, I was sitting down talking with a couple of brothers when another guy walked up and said one of the most ignorant things I believe I've ever heard in my life. We were talking about family, life, and our plans for when we get out. It was actually a very positive conversation, which is something you rarely get in a place like this. So this brother walks up and says: Life is about money, drugs, and hoes. (Excuse my language, and I apologize to all women for using this word in my book.) But it came from someone else's mouth, and I'm just using this situation as an example of how a lot of men are just plain ignorant. Remind you this man is in his fifties and will go home in less than a year. With that ignorant mentality, he'll be back or maybe even worse. The sad part about this situation is that this brother isn't the only man in the world who thinks like this. There are men in prison, in the military, men who are free who think like this. If you are one of those men who think this way, you are ignorant, foolish, and a disgrace to all men, and you'd better change your way of thinking quick, fast and in a hurry. If you are reading this and it offends you, then you need to check yourself. It breaks my heart to hear brothers talk like this, but it also pisses me off that a lot of times, guys are so stuck in their ignorant ways that they don't even want advice. They won't listen or attempt to change their thinking. These are the type of brothers that are lost, and a lot of times are insecure. Every man wants to be treated with respect and like a man, but when you have an ignorant way of thinking, nobody is going to treat you with respect. You don't even respect yourself, so how can you expect someone else to respect you? You'd better wake up and get your mind right, brother. When you look in the mirror at yourself every day, you know whether you are ignorant or foolish. How many men can look in the mirror and call themselves men? Age doesn't make you a man, money doesn't make you a man, and material things don't make you a man. Knowledge, wisdom, understanding, and responsibility are a few things that make you a man, and even those don't make you a man completely. You can be the smartest brother alive and not have your priorities together. Priorities play a major part in manhood. If you don't have your priorities in order, your life is in shambles anyway. There ain't no need to go out and buy a $500 outfit to impress your homies or this woman you are taking out if your rent is due this month. You are ignorant or foolish and don't have your priorities together. Do you believe a woman wants a man who doesn't have his stuff together? Don't no real women want an ignorant man first and foremost. If she does, she's ignorant herself and y'all are headed towards a dead end. Ignorance is the enemy of humanity. If you look ignorance up in the dictionary, it says: lacking education or knowledge, unaware or uninformed. Brothers, be mindful of the things that come out of your mouth. The tongue is the deadliest body part you have. A lot of times, we say things out of our mouths without even thinking, and it all boils down to ignorance. In the bible it says, no human being can tame the tongue, it is unruly evil, full of deadly poison (James Ch 3 V 8). A lot of people are in the grave today because they couldn't control their tongues. Brothers, we have a bad habit of referring to our women using derogatory terms. How would you feel if a man disrespected your mother or daughter, calling her her name? I see it every day here where I am. When the females come into the dorms, the brothers are constantly disrespecting them. I pulled one brother to the side and asked him what if that was your sister working here and someone disrespected her? His response was I will check them. You see, though, how can he check someone for calling his sister out of her name when he calls someone else's sister, daughter or mother out of their name on a daily basis? He is being hypocritical, and it isn't just brothers in prison. It's brothers all over the world, but once you become aware and inform brothers, and you continue to do it, then you are ignorant. Do you have a daughter? Let me explain something to you. When you have a little girl, you should feel something in your heart. Something should move you to the point that your entire outlook on women will change. You should become more mindful and aware of how you talk to and treat women. This is because you have a little girl now, and you can't imagine a man degrading your little angel. Don't get me wrong, now we as men love our sons just as much, but we are men, and we know the things that girls/women must go through in life due to ignorant boys/men. Earlier in the book, I was talking about karma. That karma doesn't always have to come back on you. If you are degrading women, then that karma could come back on your daughter. Brothers, it's time to snap out of that ignorant mentality that a lot of us are stuck in. We are leaders, teachers, and heads of the household. We have so much potential to be great men, but we must wise up and stop being ignorant. I'm challenging you right now to stop degrading and disrespecting our women. Get with one of your homeboys and put up some type of incentive. For example, every time you refer to a woman in a derogatory term, you gotta give $10 or do 50 pushups. I guarantee that after you have kicked out over $100 or done about 500 push-ups, you'll be mindful of the ignorant stuff that comes out of your mouth. Also, challenge your homeboy as well and help him get out of his ignorant state of mind. Now, if this doesn't apply to you, then I salute you, brother. I know there is something that you do that you could work on. So, work on it, brother, in the same way. Remember when I said, "Ignorance is the enemy of humanity"?

Chapter Fourteen
TRUTH & HONESTY VS. LIES & DECEIT

A lot of people say that they can handle the truth. They say that the truth will set you free. Also, when you were growing up, did your parents ever say If you had just told the truth, I wouldn't have to beat you? How many times has your woman asked you something and you lied? A lot of people say that they want to know the truth, but when you present it to them, they can't handle it. Let me give you a scenario. Let's say that you are married to a beautiful wife. One day, you go out to the grocery store to pick up something, and you run across the most beautiful woman you've ever laid eyes on. Y'all get to talking and automatically, there is an electrifying spark between the two of you. You can also feel sexual energy, so y'all exchange numbers and go your separate ways. A few days go by, then she calls, and the conversation picks up right where it left off. Eventually, y'all meet up and start to have sex. She knows you are married, but it doesn't matter because she's attracted to you. Your wife starts to hear the rumors that's going around about you having an affair with such and such. So, she confronts you with it, and instead of you telling her the truth, you deny it. Being the loving and wonderful husband that you are, she takes your word and drops the subject. A couple of months go by, and such and such calls your phone and tells you that y'all need to talk. She tells you she is pregnant with your child. Your wife confronts you a second time because now she's heard that you have impregnated another woman. Once again, you deny it. You think to yourself, I can figure something out before the baby is born. (What is there to figure out, brother?) She drops in again, and eventually the child is born, and your wife finds out that the baby is yours. Depending on your wife, the marriage is over, and y'all are headed down the road to a nasty divorce. Do you believe things would've been different if you had been honest with your wife from the beginning when she confronted you? If you had been truthful and honest, could y'all have worked it out? By lying and deceiving your wife, obviously, you felt like she couldn't handle the truth. Also, you didn't respect her enough to tell her the truth. Maybe you thought you would love her. I don't know what the case may be. But in the end, you lost her anyway because you lied. Brothers' truth and honesty will always outweigh lies and deceit. First, when you met that woman in the store, you shouldn't have let it get as far as it did by exchanging numbers with her. It doesn't matter how many sparks were flying or how big a connection you felt towards her. When you exchanged numbers with her, you already started the process of cheating. You knew she was going to call or vice versa, and that it would lead to sex. There is always a chance that sex will lead to pregnancy or something even worse. The problem with us as men we think we are so slick. That our doggish ways are not going to catch up to us. But guess what? They always do, it doesn't matter if it's two years from now or two months from now. It will eventually catch up. Let's go back to the scenario, though. When your wife first confronted you, if you were honest, a lot of things could have been avoided. Of course, she would've been pissed and hurt, but y'all could've gotten through it together. After all, isn't that what marriage is about? Working things out for better or worse. Maybe you were afraid your wife couldn't handle the truth. That could've been the case, but that's your wife, and you always owe her the truth. It doesn't matter if it hurts or not; the truth is always the right route to take. Let's say that the roles were reversed and your wife got pregnant by another man. Wouldn't you forgive her? If you answer yes, you are telling a damn lie, and the truth ain't in you. Can't no man in his right state of mind would accept the fact that another man was inside of his woman. So why do you expect your wife to accept that you were inside another woman? We must get out of that selfish state of mind and take our wedding vows more serious, brothers. We must stop lying, stop trying to be sneaky. Marriage is a lifetime commitment, brothers, and we must uphold and honor that no matter what. It's so easy for people to just throw away what they worked so hard to build, and I just don't understand it. What happened to that old-fashioned love? I remember when people used to be married at forty and fifty years and still be strong. When are we going to get back to that? I didn't write this chapter with the intention of exposing anybody for whatever lies you may be telling your partner. I wrote this chapter honestly because I wanted to help somebody's marriage out there that may be headed toward destruction. It's time to stop lying and deceiving each other and keep it real. You didn't marry that woman for nothing, brother. Obviously, y'all were in love, and you must go back to what made y'all fall in love if you have started lying and cheating. In the end, nobody wins. Not you, not her, and especially the kids if y'all have any. Your wife is your queen, so treat her as royalty. If, for some reason, you do come across a female that you are considering cheating on your wife for. Be a man and nip it in the bud before it goes that far. Talk to your wife and be honest with her. Explain to her what made you almost cheat, and y'all can work on it. I know it sounds crazy, but brothers, if you are truthful and honest, it will carry your marriage a long way and it will ALWAYS outweigh lies and deceit.

Chapter Fifteen

DISTRACTIONS

It is easy for us as men to lose focus and get sidetracked because there are so many distractions involved. A distraction can be anything from family and friends to television and partying. It is so easy to lose focus on your long-term goals and what it is in life that you are trying to accomplish because we are easily distracted. Take, for example, the brothers in prison. You've been sentenced, so now you are in prison for whatever amount of time you have. Instead of going to school, getting a GED or taking up some type of trade, a lot of brothers come to prison and get caught up in the "prison politics" or the distractions. They sit around all day doing nothing to become a better man to society when they are released. They still have the same mentality that landed them in prison. All day they sit around gossiping, watching TV, playing games or getting high. Just to name a few. All the things are distractions and don't help you grow. The brothers who aren't incarcerated are sitting around playing video games, on Facebook, gossiping, partying or getting high, just to name a few. I understand that we do have hobbies. That's part of being a human, but you must have constructive hobbies, and you can't let those hobbies become a distraction. When you start neglecting your family, and I don't necessarily mean neglecting them like turning your back on them. You can neglect your family by not showing them attention, not listening when they need that ear or shoulder to cry on. That's when the problem comes in, brother. "What you don't do for her, she'll find somebody else who can". I know you all heard that saying before. It is true, and a woman will seek that attention elsewhere if you stop giving it to her. We, as men, allow all types of distractions to ruin our relationships. I'm talking about so many simple things that can easily be avoided. Take work, for instance. You are constantly working six, sometimes seven, days a week, and by the time you get home, you are exhausted, so you don't spend any time with your wife or kids. Work has become a distraction. Yeah, I know you have to work in order to pay bills, but sometimes you must take a break. Instead of working 72 hours every week, try to narrow it down some. Take some vacation time and do something with your family. Work is mandatory, but when it becomes a distraction, then there is a problem. If your child is in school and the teacher is in front of the class explaining the solution to a problem, but your child is on the phone texting or on the internet, they are distracted and won't be able to explain the solution to the problem that the teacher just explained. So, when it's time for the test, they fail. The teacher calls you and explains to you that your son or daughter isn't paying attention in class, and now you want to punish them in some form or fashion. You are wrong and a hypocrite if you are one of the brothers who is distracted. How can you tell your kids to pay attention if you don't pay attention? You have to teach your kids by example through your actions. Distractions come in so many different forms and at all types of times. People get distracted while driving down the road, which causes accidents. A lot of guys in prison look at their families as a distraction. I know it sounds crazy, but it's true. They feel that they must sever ties with their family in order to get through their time. In their mind, their family is an emotional distraction that could cause them to lose focus and get hurt. It's not something I agree with, but everybody has their own way of doing things. As a man who's currently incarcerated, I don't feel that you should refer to your family as a distraction, but that's another conversation in its entirety. I will say this: if you are currently incarcerated and you are reading this, don't push your family away because you consider them a distraction. This is a very dark place, and you need your family and loved ones so you can have some type of motivation. End of discussion! Brothers, as men, it is our responsibility not to allow any type of distraction to interfere with our family. It doesn't matter what it is. You must be mindful and become aware if you have been distracted. It's not too late, brothers! Remember, "Distractions can lead to disasters." When was the last time you took your family on vacation? When was the last time you planned an outing and followed up on it with your family? There are so many places we can take our family to get away from all the hassle and stress. There are so many extracurricular activities that we can do with our family if we just take the time to do them. If you don't have the money and can't afford a vacation, it's all good. There is still plenty to do that won't cost you an arm and a leg. Take your family bowling, skating, to the beach, etc. You can even take your family to the park and have a picnic. These are just a few examples of things to do as a family to take you away from those distractions. Don't allow the distractions to cause you to lose your family. Believe it happens, brothers.

Chapter Sixteen
POSITIVE VS NEGATIVE
(MIRROR, MIRROR ON THE WALL)

———— •••• ————

Do you know anybody who is always negative and always looking for the worst possible outcome? Are you this person, or are you a person who is optimistic and, no matter what the situation, you take something positive from it? This chapter coincides a little bit with chapter six (karma), but it isn't exactly the same. Often, we are quick to expect the worst out of any and all situations. I know you are familiar with the saying "prepare for the best but expect the worse". In my opinion, that is one of the dumbest sayings I've heard. Go back and look at that saying and then repeat it out loud. It is a contradiction. You can't prepare for the best but expect the worse. That is two different attitudes (positive and negative), and you can't be positive and negative at the same time. That's just not how things work, brother. Either you are going to think positive, or you are going to think negative. A lot of times, when I'm talking to my lady, she'll tell me about certain situations that come up in her life. Sometimes there are bad things and sometimes there are good things, but when the bad things come up, she always finds something good out of that bad situation. That is because she knows she must keep a positive attitude, despite whatever the circumstances may be. Don't ever expect the worst, brother; always prepare for the best and expect the best. Once you have expected the worst, you are going to get the worst because you are in a negative mind frame. So, the first step is to get out of that negative mind frame. If you are constantly in a negative mind frame, then those are the type of people that you are going to attract. If you are constantly in a negative mind frame, then don't be surprised or wonder why people are always negative towards you. You are attracting that negative energy into your life. A lot of brothers here are always negative about everything. Take, for instance, they want their woman to write them. So, she writes, and when they get the letter, it isn't long enough for them, or they want their family to put money in their account. When their family sends the money, now they are complaining it isn't enough. A few days ago, one of the younger brothers here received a money receipt indicating that his family had sent him money. Instead of him being thankful, he says, "Man, it's about time they sent me some damn money, it took long enough". I told him, instead of being negative and complaining, brother, why don't you call your people and tell them thank you? He looked at me strangely for a quick second and then went and called his family. My point is, this just doesn't happen to men in prison. Men all over the world are complaining and finding fault in something. We have got to get out of that negative mentality period. It doesn't matter who you are or where you are; you've got to snap out of it. Especially if you are going to make some progress in this lifetime. I love to tell the brothers to look in the mirror and talk to themselves. Tighten yourself up and tell yourself what the negative characteristics are that you need to work on. If you are constantly thinking negatively, find out what it is you can do to change that. What or who is causing you to have these negative thoughts? I guarantee that if you look in the mirror and look, you'll find the solution to your problems.

When I was younger, my grandmother used to always listen to gospel music. There was this one song that always stood out to me growing up, and even to this day, it still has a positive effect on my life. In the song, they say, "sweep around your own front door before you try to sweep around mine". How can I tell you that you aren't living a righteous life if I'm not living righteous myself? I must first look at myself and clean myself up before I can even attempt to give any advice. If I am always on a negative level, I can't tell you to be more positive. In the bible, Jesus knew that the faults we see in other people are the faults that he sees in ourselves. He spoke on it in detail when he said "why do you see that speck that is in your brother's eye, but do not notice the log that is in your own eye? How can you say to your brother, "Brother let me take out the speck that is in your eye, when you yourself do not take the log out of your own eye, and then you will see clearly to take out the speck that is in your brother's eye" (Luke 6: 41,42)

Once we get that speck of dust out of our own eyes, brothers, then we can try to help the next brother change. I didn't say judge the next man, I said help the brother. Often, people are so ignorant that they don't believe that they need to change. Brothers, we can only change ourselves. You can't change the next man; you can give advice and encourage the brother, but changing is entirely up to him. Don't point out the next man's faults; then you are judging that brother. Take me for example! A lot of people are going to look at this book and say, "Who does this dude think he is to put out a book judging me?" But I didn't pass this book out to judge anybody. Obviously, though, if you are in your feelings about this book, then you need to tighten yourself up. See, I've looked in the mirror and I no longer liked what I saw, I know it's brothers out there with the potential to be so much better, only if they would look in the mirror. That's why I put this book out to inspire and motivate every man out there who is willing to change. Don't be that brother who puts his pride in the way of everything. Look in that mirror and recognize your flaws and work on yourself. Everything starts with you. Change that negative attitude toward life into a positive attitude, brother. Our women, our kids, our families need us. It can only happen once you recognize the man in the mirror!

Chapter Seventeen
OVERCOMING ADVERSITY

In life, things aren't going to always go as you planned. There are going to be roadblocks, trials, tribulations, and adversity. We are so quick to call on God when things are suddenly going wrong. But what about when things are going well? How many times do we acknowledge him then? We go through things in life that either make us stronger or break us completely down. It is how you recover and overcome those things that truly determines the man that you are. One thing I know for sure is that after it rains, the sun will eventually come out and shine. Brothers, we must remain strong and overcome all adversity that may come our way. Being a man isn't easy at all. Being a man comes with a lot of duties, obligations, and responsibilities. At times it can be stressful, and at times I know you want to give up, but in the end, when it's all said and done, all your hard work and determination pay off. Who wants everything to come easy anyway? If everything were easy in life, where would the excitement be? There wouldn't be much excitement; it would get boring quickly. So many times, when things aren't going our way, we question God. Not only do we question God, but sometimes we might even question our own manhood. I know how it feels to question your own manhood. Every morning, I listen to the Steve

Harvey morning show, and right at six, he gives words of encouragement and inspiration. Then, right before he goes off, he drops some more jewels on the world. No matter what I'm going through, I always hear Steve Harvey's voice giving me words of inspiration, and I take that adversity that comes my way and turn it into inspiration and motivation. There is an old story that I read in a book about this old man who was always complaining and praying to God about his sufferings, about his burdens, about the adversity he was going through. For years, this old man prayed to God about these things. One night, he has a dream, but this isn't an ordinary dream. This dream is vivid, clear and the most beautiful dream he's had. In his dream, he is surrounded by millions of people. Suddenly, God appears in the sky and says, "Everyone has been praying to me about their burdens, sufferings, and adversities. Some of you even say that you are willing to take someone else's problems to get rid of your own. All of you have bags in front of you. Take your problems and place them in that bag, then go put your bag up against the wall". So, everybody takes their bag and places it against the wall. God then tells everybody to pick up a bag that they want. The old man ran straight to his own bag before anybody else could pick it up his bag. When he looked around, he saw everyone running towards their own bags as well. The thing is, when everyone lined their bags up against the wall, they got a peek into the next person's bags, and they realized that despite what they were going through, somebody else was going through something worse. Brothers, I use this story as my inspiration as well because I know for a fact that there is somebody's situation way worse than mine. The same thing applies to you as well. So instead of constantly complaining and pouting about it, do something to make it better. Don't ponder on your situation, because your situation isn't anything compared to some people's. Adversities are going to come at you from all different angles. Especially when you are trying to do right and change. A lot of people look at it as a test.

Whether or not you pass that test is entirely up to you. The main thing is to stand firm. I tell my woman all the time to stay firm and be consistent. The other day, when I was talking on the phone with her, I could feel her spirits were down. We have this connection where one can feel in their spirit when the other is down. So, at first, I'm thinking that I've said something to discourage her. I ask her what's going on, Baby. I can feel something is going on with you. She then tells me that she has been feeling down because she is trying to get another job, and nobody seems to be trying to hire her. It really has her down, and she just feels like nothing is going right. I tell her that she must snap out of that funk first and foremost. If one door closes in your face, keep knocking until somebody eventually lets you in. Some things just aren't meant to be. There is always something better in place for you. You must find it. That goes for anybody in life. Brothers don't get down, depressed, or discouraged just because one thing doesn't work for us. Eventually, something way better will come through. It's about overcoming that adversity, it's about staying consistent and putting in that work to get where you want to be. Just don't take anything for granted. When that opportunity comes, take full advantage of it. Adversity is only a minor steppingstone. Once you overcome it, the sky is the limit.

Chapter Eighteen
SELF HEALTH

Brothers, it's time that we wake up and realize the importance of our health. When was the last time you went to the doctor for a physical exam? A lot of times, we don't even go to the doctors for checkups. We wait until the last minute when something is ailing us. Maybe what's ailing us could've been avoided if we had gone to the doctor for a monthly check-up. Men are dying younger these days, and it isn't just from street violence. Men are having heart attacks and strokes more frequently now because we aren't mindful of our health. We are poisoning our bodies with the food we take in daily. It might be good, and don't feel like it's doing anything, but in the long run, what we are eating is slowly killing us. Also, we aren't doing any physical activities such as exercising, jogging, or playing pick-up games. Anything to keep our bodies in shape and healthy. We have become complacent, and it's not healthy at all. I'm not saying that you must become a vegetarian or become a fitness trainer. I'm saying that we as men must be more mindful. I'm pretty sure every man wants to see his kids grow up and spend time with his grandkids and possibly great-grandkids as well. For this to happen, we must start taking better care of ourselves. How often do you eat out at fast food restaurants? A lot of us eat out three to four times a week, if not more. I'm not trying to knock fast food restaurants, but you can do your own research and see that eating out isn't healthy for you. A lot of our health problems could be avoided if only we slowed down a little bit and became aware. Do you remember when you were younger and your mother or grandmother would make you eat all your vegetables? We would cry, try to give them to the dog, sneak and throw them away. Anything we could do to get out of eating those vegetables, but we were quick to drink that Kool-Aid or eat that cake or any type of junk food. Our parents/grandparents made us eat those vegetables because they knew the importance of eating healthier. We were young and thought our people were wrong for making us eat healthy, but what they were trying to do was instill in us the importance of healthy eating. How often do you get on your kids about what they are eating? I'm pretty sure you make them eat their vegetables and everything before you allow them to satisfy that sweet tooth. Don't be a hypocrite, though, brother. What are you going to say when your kids ask you why you are not eating healthy? So, practice what you preach! In this chapter, I'm not trying to sit here and act like I'm a dietician because I'm not. I just want the brothers to realize the importance of their health. If you are healthy physically, mentally, and spiritually, you'll perform better in all that you do. It could be work, sex or anything. It is a proven fact that exercise relieves stress. A lot of times, when we are stressed out, we have the tendency to take our frustrations out on our family. I'm not talking about physically (although some men do). I'm talking about verbally or emotionally. We've had a long day at work and come home, and anything the kids do irritates us, or if your wife is supposed to have done something but didn't, you feel that's reason enough to take your stress out on her. Brothers, go hit the gym and take your stress and frustrations out on the weights, or you can go to the room and meditate. Meditation is a major stress reliever as well. It gives you peace of mind, also. It takes time and patience, though. The first few times you try it, you might get frustrated and think you can't do it; however, if you stick with it and I guarantee you'll be more at peace and less stressed. All of this coincides with your health because stress literally kills. We are human, so naturally at times we are going to stress. You must keep it to a minimum if you plan on being around for a while. Working that stress out through meditation and exercise. If you do the research, you'll see that more men die due to an inadequate level of physical activity as opposed to those who exercise regularly. Take care of your health, brothers. Your family needs you to be healthy and in good shape.

Chapter Nineteen
PHYSICAL VS. VERBAL ABUSE

———◦•◦•———

At the beginning of this book (chapter one, matter of fact), I mentioned how when I was younger, I used to witness my mother being physically abused by different men in her life. As I was writing this book, I felt in my spirit that I needed to dedicate a chapter touching on domestic violence because there are millions of so-called men out there who physically abuse women. If you are one of those men that I'm referring to, it's time to put an end to it. You need help, and I pray that this chapter will hit a soft spot for you, and you'll go get the help you need. If you are one of the men who used to physically abuse women, and you've changed, I'm proud of you for changing, but you still need to read this. If you are a man who has never put his hands on a woman intending to hurt her physically, I salute you, but you need to read this as well. Maybe you have a homeboy or a family member who is physically abusive towards his woman, or maybe you have a female relative who has been in an abusive relationship or is currently involved with a man who is abusive. Before I go any further in this chapter, I want to give you some actual facts. Fact number one: The top reasons why men physically abuse women are: alcohol/drugs, anger management, insecurities, and control issues. Fact number two: In the past twelve months, fewer than 1/3 (28.8 percent) of men were arrested for domestic abuse. (This is only the cases that were reported) Fact number three: More women (the actual victims) have been identified as being charged more than men who are doing the abusing. I could go on giving you mind-blowing facts about domestic abuse, but I want to touch on these three in general before I touch on these facts, though. I want you to understand that domestic violence isn't just happening among men and women. It's happening with boys and girls (teenagers, to be more specific). Back when I was in high school, there was a very young, pretty girl whose name I can't disclose, but she ended up getting involved with a young guy who had insecurity issues. I remember I used to hear from the other students how he was physically abusive towards her and how he would mistreat and humiliate her in front of other people. One day, as we were changing periods, I headed to my next class when I saw a crowd gathered around. Naturally, I walked over to see what was going on, and there they were. He and she in the middle, surrounded by everyone. He is insulting her with words, and she is crying, covering her face. Apparently, he had just bought her some new shoes, and he was upset because he had seen her talking to another guy. He made her take her shoes off and walk around barefooted the rest of the day. Brothers, can you imagine if some young punk mistreating and humiliating your little girl like that? A lot of us would more than likely catch a charge, honestly. So, pay attention to what's going on in your kids' lives as well, because that could be your little girl or it could even be your son. Trust me, it's going on with our youth as well.

Alcohol/drugs: Men who physically abuse women are constantly trying to make up excuses to justify why they put their hands on their women. Often, alcohol and drugs do play a major role for the most part, but at the end of the day, it's still inexcusable. If you know that you abuse your woman when you are under the influence, why not quit indulging in whatever it is that's causing you to hurt her? If you have a drinking or drug problem, there are programs out there that you can get help from. You must want help, though, brothers. You must want to change; it starts with you. When you are drinking or doing drugs, depending on how much, a lot of times you aren't in the right frame of mind. So, when you sober up and realize what you've done, you are begging for forgiveness. But if you are constantly doing the same thing over again, then you have a serious problem, and you need to get help before you end up hurting her a lot worse than you already have. Alcohol and drugs aren't an excuse, period!

Anger management: So now your excuse is that you have anger problems. Once again, that is a pathetic excuse. Just like they have classes for alcoholics and drug addicts, they have anger management classes. Whatever you are angry about, it still doesn't give you the right to put your hands on your woman. If you want to relieve some anger by putting your hands on something or somebody, go to the gym. More specifically, go to the boxing gym and relieve that stress. Your woman isn't a punching bag at all. You have a problem if you think otherwise. Find an anger management class and get there quick before you do something you can't take back. Anger management isn't an excuse, period!!!

Insecurities: The worst characteristic, in my opinion, for a man to have is being insecure. Insecurities open so many other negative characteristics in a man, such as jealousy, envy, spitefulness, etc. If you can't stand to see your woman talking to another man, working with other men or being friends with other men, then you are insecure as hell. Your woman was seen talking to another man, and now you put your hands on her. You are a coward, and somebody needs to put their hands on you. If you are treating your woman like the queen she is, taking care of home and satisfying all her needs, you have no reason to be insecure. If you know that you are doing what you are supposed to be doing, then you don't have to worry about another man taking your place. Talk to your woman if you get the feeling that she is unhappy. Inquire about what you can do to make it right, brothers. Don't allow your insecurities to surface and ruin your relationship or turn you into somebody that your female companion despises. Communication is the key!!! Insecurities aren't an excuse, period!!!

Control issues: Last but certainly not least, you have men that has control issues. Maybe growing up as a kid, this type of man never had any say-so with his friends, or maybe this type of man is insecure, and he must have total control over his woman. I don't know what the case may be, but it can't be justified. The fact of the matter is, you have no right to try and control your woman. You can't tell her what she can or can't do. She isn't your child; she isn't your slave. You have absolutely no authority over her. If you are this type of man, then you need help as well. You don't want to be controlled, so don't try to be a controller. Control issues aren't an excuse, period!!!

In the past 12 months, 28.8% of men have been arrested for domestic violence. That is a very low number, which tells me that men are getting away with this. How is it possible that more women get arrested for domestic violence when they are the victims? There is something wrong with that picture, brothers. As men, we must step up and let our voices be heard pertaining to this issue. We must let our presence be felt. If we are the ones mistreating, abusing and running over our women, then we are the ones who can fix it. It's time to step up and not only bring awareness to the situation but also find a solution to this problem. True indeed, I know we can't control what goes on at every household, but you can control what goes on in yours. You can help bring awareness to a male friend who may be abusive towards his woman. It doesn't necessarily have to be physical abuse either. Verbal abuse is just as bad as physical abuse. If you are disrespecting, talking to your woman like she is nothing. That isn't right at all. You are wrong, and you need to check yourself, brother. It is our duty as a man to uplift, inspire, and motivate our women. We weren't put here to abuse our women physically or verbally. Build your woman's confidence up, don't kill her self-esteem. She is your better half, and if you don't get it together, she will eventually find the courage to leave you and move on to a man who will treat her as the queen that she is. Let's get it together, brothers. One positive change within yourself could have a domino effect, and you could motivate other men. Love your woman, honor, respect, cherish and grow with your woman. If you call yourself a man, then act like it. Be a man not only through your words, but through your actions. If you are one of the ones who have these issues that were addressed in these chapters, get some help, brother and get it fast. By getting help, you are putting forth the effort to change, and you realize you have a problem. If you are one of the men who have these issues but won't do anything to change your problem, you are a coward, you are the lowest scum of the earth, and you will get what you deserve eventually. Don't be this man, brothers!!!

Chapter Twenty
WORKING MAN VS LAZY MAN

There are two types of men in this world, if you ask me. You have your working men, and then you have your lazy men. Hopefully, if you are reading this book, you are the working man, but if, for some reason, you are reading this book and you are the lazy man, at least you have taken the initiative to see what I'm talking about, and if anything pertains to you, you can better yourself and your situation. I'm pretty sure that if you took a poll and asked 100 women, would they rather have a working man or a lazy man? All 100 women would definitely say a working man. If, for some odd reason, someone says a lazy man, then she might be crazy or have her own personal issues. Whatever the case may be, something is definitely off balance there. If you are the type of man who is laid up, unemployed and depending on your woman to take care of you, then you are definitely categorized as the lazy man. You think that you are going to continue to get by based on good sex alone. Eventually, that woman is going to get sick and tired of you and your sex. If you are not bringing anything to the table, that lustful state of mind that you are caught up in will fade away. Sooner rather than later, she is going to realize that she can get good sex (if not better sex than what you are giving) from a man who actually has his things together and is bringing a lot more to the table than what you are bringing. It really doesn't make no sense for you to call yourself a grown man but all you do is sit around and waste your life. You are a man age-wise wise but that's as far as your manhood goes. If you are offended by my words, then so be it. Obviously, I've hit a nerve, and the truth is settling within you. I'm not going to spend much time talking about the lazy man, cause if you don' have it together by now, chances are you aren't going to get it together. This is not to discourage you by any means. I hope it motivates you to get up and get your stuff together, then maybe you can call me out and inform me that you did what I said you wouldn't do.

Now, as far as the working man is concerned. First, I salute you and I tip my hat to you for being a working man, but that doesn't make you any better than the next man. By working, you are doing what a man is supposed to do. It feels good to know that you are a man who takes care of his home and provides for his family. You are supposed to feel good, and nobody can take that feeling away from you because you earned the right to feel that way, but at the same time, don't look down on the next man (even the lazy man). Maybe you can help motivate that lazy man.

Often, I sit back and listen to these young brothers talk, and I just shake my head in disappointment. A lot of guys these days don't know anything at all about hard work. They call themselves men, but in actuality, they are still babies. They don't know what it's like to take care of a home. Back in the days, our grandparents had to work hard to earn a living. Every dime they made, they put into the work for it. I'm talking about hard labor. If you took 90% of these guys today and put them in a tobacco field or any type of hard labor jobs, they would quit in a couple of hours, if not sooner. Don't misinterpret what I'm saying now. Just because you have an office job in the AC doesn't make you lazy. You are still working. My point is that a lot of guys just don't have it in them to work. They would rather take the easy way out by hustling or depending on a woman. For you to be successful, you must put in the proper work. You can pray and ask God to do things for you, but you can't just sit around and not do anything and expect results. It's the same thing with success. You've got to get up off your behind and go get it. Anything else is inexcusable!

Chapter Twenty-One
LEADERS AND FOLLOWERS

Are you a leader or are you a follower? Before you answer this question, I want you to really think about it. Every man wants to be a leader, but before you become a great leader, you must be a follower. It is natural for a man to want to be the leader, the shot caller, alpha male or whatever you want to call it. Every man wants to have this title to his name, but every man just doesn't have what it takes to be that leader. You must have certain qualities, and not only that, you must be able to back up what you say and lead by example. Nobody is trying to follow a so-called leader if that leader isn't living up to his words. You can't just talk the talk; you must walk the walk, even in our relationships with our women. Your woman wants you to take the lead. She wants to follow your lead, but if you don't have that fire in you or that spunk that women look for, she isn't going to follow you anywhere. As a man, we are born to be natural leaders, but a lot of us can't handle the responsibility of being a leader.

First and foremost, if you are a leader, you must be able to think. If you can't think, then not only are you not a leader, but you are in a world of trouble. Being able to think is one of the most important qualities of a great leader. Keep it real with yourself. Who in their right mind wants to or is going to follow somebody who can't think? NOBODY!!! You must be able to think on all levels as well. You can't just be a one-track mind thinker, brother. A lot of wars have been won because the right person calling the shots can think. Wars that are avoided because the person in charge thinks they are the best wars won. There are different types of wars as well. Not just wars on the battlefield. Life is a war. If you can think and win the war against life, that means you have the potential to be a great leader. Life is the greatest war you will ever encounter because every day of our lives, we are faced with different situations. Depending on how we do or don't react to these situations determines whether we have leadership abilities. If we move or react off impulse or our emotions, that could be very detrimental not only to us but to our families as well. If we sit back and think and/or plan everything out, we'll get better results, and that's what makes us leaders. Everything we need is deep within us, brothers. To be a great leader, you don't have to read a hundred books. You don't have to go on the internet. All you must do is look within. Pray and meditate on it. It may seem far-fetched, but trust me. If you search and look deep enough, you'll find it. Now I'm not telling you not to read. I encourage all brothers to read. There is a lot of knowledge in certain books, but if you are truly looking to be a great leader, it's already in you. It's just up to you and you alone to discover it. We have become so complacent as men to the point where we don't want to elevate to that next level. We have become content with where we are in life, but if you are a leader, you are never content with just settling. You want to continue to grow and become an even greater leader. You want those who follow you to embrace and be honored to have you as their leader. Earlier, I mentioned that before you become a great leader, you must be a follower. You must learn from experience as well. Everybody that are leader all over the world was a follower at some point in their lives. A lot of brothers are so prideful, they think they aren't followers, but I'm here to tell you that you don't just jump off the porch as a leader. It doesn't matter who you are. We don't know everything there is to know about leadership. Someone must teach you or school you, but guess what? The person who teaches you had a teacher as well, and so forth. So, if you are one of those brothers who think you are automatically a leader and that you don't have to listen to anybody, you are a fool, and you'd better recognize this flaw in your way of thinking. A little bit of practice will carry you a long way.

Chapter Twenty~Two
SACRIFICES/COMPROMISING

Whether you are a father, a husband, a friend, etc., eventually you will have to make some type of sacrifice. Eventually, you are going to have to compromise as well. That sacrifice could be something you have to give up for the sake of your wife or children. Regardless of what the case may be, as a man, you will one day have to make sacrifices for your kids as well as your wife. If you can recall earlier in the book, I was talking about how when we were young, our mothers had to make sacrifices for us so we could get that new pair of shoes or whatever we wanted. A lot of women will sacrifice it all to make sure that their kids have food on the table, clothes on their backs and a roof over their head. We as men need to take a page out of our women's book and start making sacrifices. The thing, though, about men is that we are so egotistical and we allow our pride to get in our way. So that will have to be the very first sacrifice we make. Take that pride and ego and do away with it first and foremost. Once we set that aside, we will realize how easy making sacrifices will be. You might think that having pride, being egotistical, making sacrifices and compromising don't have anything to do with one another, but in actuality, they do.

How can you sit down and compromise with your wife if you have pride issues? How can you make peace with another man if you have an inflated ego? Do you see my point now? It all coincides once you sit down and think about it. When it comes to compromising and living under the same roof with a woman, you'd better be able to compromise, or you'll get run out of that house quick. People who have been married 30,40,50 years are still together and in love because they know how to compromise, and they've made plenty of sacrifices. Being able to compromise and make sacrifices is both a part of being a man. If anybody else tells you differently, they don't know what they are talking about. At the end of the day, just like everything else in life, it all starts with you. You must want to work on changing. You must be the one to decide to put that pride and ego aside. I can go on and on telling you to set it aside. Your friends, wife, and family can tell you the same thing, but if you don't take heed and implement it, then we are all wasting our time and energy. So many relationships fail these days because people don't know how to compromise. Believe it or not, it is simple. Have you heard of the phrase "you have to give to get?" That's really all that compromising is. You give a little bit, then you get a little bit. I was talking to my woman the other day, and we were talking about the "what ifs" when I get home. She is so worried that once I get there, we might not like living with one another, even though we are deep in love. She says that living with someone is totally different than just coming over for the night. She gave me the idea for this chapter as far as the title goes. So, I explained to her that if we are in love the way we say we are, then we will be alright because we will sit down and compromise with one another. Something we started early in our relationship is doing monthly evaluations of where we are as a couple. Every month on our anniversary date, we will question one another. For example, I'll ask her what I need to work on, or how she feels about our relationship right now at this point. Those are just a few questions I might ask her, and she'll respond and then ask me whatever it is that she wants to ask. My point is that through communicating our issues or what not, we find a way to compromise. If there is something I need to work on, she'll tell me, and we will go from there. Love and life are about sacrifices and compromise. We as men must do a better job in these areas of our lives. Once we start to compromise with our women, we will see positive changes instantly in our relationship, so let's tighten up, brothers and get it together. Sit down with your woman and find out what it is you need to work on. I promise you that when she tells you and you make that change, your relationship will be a lot smoother.

Chapter Twenty-Three
DEALING WITH CHANGES

As you grow into the man that God created you to be, many changes will happen in your life. Hopefully, after reading this book, a change will happen in your life. How many times has someone told you, "Boy, you better change your ways or else…." How many times has your lady told you that you need to change? When you become a real man, that should automatically come with change, brothers. Let me warn you, though, that when you decide to make that change, you will lose some so-called friends. You will even make some enemies. Those so-called friends will even become enemies, but they were enemies all along if they are mad because you changed for the better. I know you've heard of the saying "misery loves company". Oftentimes, those friends that you think have your best interest at heart, only want to see you down and miserable, just like them. So, when they see the change in you for the better, they don't like it at all and will do or say all they can to convince you that change isn't good. 99% of the time, brothers, change is always for the good. How do you think a woman looks at it? Let me be the first to tell you that no woman wants a man who isn't willing or ready for change. A grown woman wants a grown man, period. If you are the type of man who wants to someday settle down and have a family, then eventually you will have to change those boyish ways. All of that hanging in the streets, coming home late at night, isn't what a grown woman wants. A woman wants a sense of certainty and stability. She isn't trying to be up all night, wondering who you are, sexing, or if you are going to make it home. Back in the days when you were younger, you might've thought that was cool, but now things are way different. It's time for a change. As men, there comes a point in our lives where we must let go of ignorance. I heard somebody before say that insanity is when you keep doing the same thing again, getting the same results, but you are expecting different results. You must change up and try something new, brothers. We must get out of that ignorant state of mind. The only way we are going to prosper is if we first change our mental state of mind. The thing with us as men is that we have trained our minds to think that certain things are cool. As boys growing up, seeds were planted in our minds. For example, we grow up thinking that it's okay to have more than one woman. We grow up thinking that it's cool to sell drugs to get that nice car, big house and pretty girl, but these are the seeds that we must change for our own future young men. We must start planting more positive and different seeds in our young kids' minds so that they will grow up and be more successful than we have been in years past. How can our youth change if we don't show them the way? When they see us, they mimic what they see. We must change our entire way of thinking if we are going to help our youth change their thinking. It all boils down to change. It's time that we, as men, take that step and accept change gracefully. It's time to grow as men mentally, emotionally, as well as spiritually. Once we make that commitment to change, we will reap the benefits and all the good that comes with change. Everything is on us, so challenge yourself to change. Do it for yourself. Don't do it for anybody else, do it for YOU!!!

Chapter Twenty-Four
FORGIVENESS

As I was writing this book, all types of ideas were running through my mind on what I wanted to title the last and final chapter. So, one day I'm reading quotes out of a book, and I see a quote that says, "Forgiveness is the final form of love". When I saw that quote, I knew that the final chapter of my book would be titled "Forgiveness". At the end of the day, when it comes to love, family, relationships, friendships, etc., people do things to us that may hurt, but for us to move forward with our lives, regardless of the situation, we must forgive. As a man, it seems that we have the biggest problem forgiving people. We can go cheat on our wives or girlfriend and expect her to forgive us, but the minute we find out another man was inside our woman, we lose our minds. We can't believe that our woman would do something like that to us. In our eyes, that is the ultimate betrayal, and we just can't accept it. We don't want to hear anything she has to say. Forgiveness is the last thing on our minds, but if we would just put that pride and ego to the side, we would know and understand that for our woman to go out and do that, obviously, she wasn't getting something from us. We must learn to forgive as men. It doesn't necessarily have to be with a woman. It could be any type of situation with a friend, coworker, family member, etc. For us to move forward, we must forgive each other. There is no need to walk around longer than necessary holding on to a grudge. Cherish your loved ones' brothers because life is short. You don't want to wake up one day and your loved one has passed on, and you never got the chance to tell them how you felt. There is too much going on in the world for us as men to be walking around stubborn. If God forgives us for everything that we do, then why can't we forgive someone for hurting us? We aren't bigger or better than God, period. So, if he can forgive you, so can you. It is time for us as men to tighten up. It is time for us to grow and be the kings we were born to be. It doesn't matter what your race, religion, or beliefs are. If you call yourself a man, I'm talking to you. MAN UP! Don't worry about the past; that is done and can't be undone. It's time to forgive yourself for the things you've done and the way you've acted before you became a man. Today is a new day; tomorrow is gone. Focus on the present and the future. Our kids need us, our women need us, our families need us. Get to know yourself, brother. It's not too late. If I offended any man with anything I've said in this book, GOOD! That means something I said struck a nerve, and it's time for you to MAN UP!!!